Life As Once We Knew It

Images of a Lost Human Epoch
By
Annie Leibovitz

First Published Worldwide as an
Ebook and Printed Volume in 2014

Photographs and Text © 2014
by
Annie Leibovitz
All Rights Reserved

Edited by Alicia Gunderne

Designed by Natasha Hill

Preface

In the beginning was the world, and the world was good. We as Mankind roamed the earth in search of things and found things to please us. But we lost our link with Mother Earth and uprooted ourselves from her. Never to return?

Within these pages I have depicted humans as part of the Natural World – as once we were.

I hope you will see within these pages the purity and invigoration of the Life Force that made you.

Annie Leibovitz New York 2014

Introduction

Annie Leibovitz is a portrait photographer She aims to express within this new collection the flowing lines and deification of the human body as seen in classical Greek and Roman sculptures

The pictures in this album were shot in England USA and Greece between 2006 and 2013

Annie Leibovitz lives in New York and London

Alicia Gunderne the editor of this album is a creative director for Framepool Photo Library in Munich Germany

Natasha Hill the designer of this book is a photographic editor and designer in her first year of study toward an MA in photography at the University of Los Angeles in California USA

The Formation of Structure

Will

Configuration

Heart or Darkness

Water Where Life

Progress, Form, Existence

Xylem

Esse is Percipi

Will and Recurrence

Geoform

Amalgamation

Gravitation

Lumen Accipe

Found

Lost

Was; A Covenant

Transmigration of Elements

Clavigera

The Synapse State

The Elements Have Changed

From Thence, The Earth Responded

The Inevitability of Carbonism

A Treatise Was Established

Now One

Tragedio

Life as One

A Change Afoot

Emergence Is Our Witness

The Green Man

Triumvir

Re-Creation

Impasse

Light

Conclave

Level

Constratum

Expansion

Now Thus

Perceptio

Lumen Accipe II

Abor Semper Vitae

Terra Unedo Tempor

Terra Minimus

Elapse

Re-Cognition

Fors

Castanum

Elapse

Re-Cognition

Fors

Castanum

Castanus

Juris Perdus

Gracium Evidus

Flux

Surveillum

Terra Timidus

Inconclavius

Rodaltus

Axius

Non-Evadus

Gamus

Regulio

Retraction

Expansion

Completion

Reorientation

Relegation

Absolution

Nuncio

Espirtus

Callis Salvator

Callis Terminus

Callis Accipe

Arcturium

Retrium

FINIS

www.ingramcontent.com/pod-product-compliance
Lightning Source LLC
Chambersburg PA
CBHW081907170526
45167CB00007B/3186